Your Financial Revolution

THE POWER OF STRATEGY

WORKBOOK

GARY KEESEE

ISBN: 978-1-945930-17-1

Printed by Free Indeed Publishers.
Distributed by Faith Life Now.

Faith Life Now
P.O. Box 779
New Albany, OH 43054
1-(888)-391-LIFE

You can reach Faith Life Now Ministries on the Internet at www.faithlifenow.com.

CONTENTS

QUESTIONS:
Fill in the blanks from your reading.

 SCRIPTURES:
Dive into the Word of God.

 THOUGHTS:
Respond to these prompts to go deeper.

 KNOW THIS:
Meditate on these important standout statements.

 **PRAYER**

INTRODUCTION
HOW TO GET THE ANSWERS YOU NEED

Years ago, I was facing some obstacles. I had a dream one night that I was standing in the desert, and in front of me was a straight road surrounded by flat sand. God said, "Walk down the road." So I began walking.

Suddenly, HUGE cement barriers began to pop up here and there and completely block one side of the road or the other so that I had to dodge them as I walked.

Then, someone came up behind me and put a blindfold on me. "How am I going to walk down the road? I can't see where I'm going!" I asked God.

"By My Spirit," He said.

Friend, that's how our lives are supposed to be lived as believers—*by His Spirit.*

Now, what does that really mean? *It means God wants to help you.*

It means He wants you to trust Him with your problems and with your questions. It means He wants you to walk in His power. You have the right to be led in life by the Spirit of God. That's a whole lot better than you trying to figure it out on your own.

See, the Bible doesn't tell you who to marry, what degree to get, or what occupation you should have. It doesn't tell you whether or not you should buy or sell a house or buy or sell your stocks, or anything like that.

But to be successful in life, you have to know those things.

God *wants* you to know those things. He really does.

See, you have access to some amazing help. The Bible tells us that the Holy Spirit is our Counselor. He's there to help you in life, in business, and in your relationships. He's there to give you new ideas and plans that will take you to incredible places you've never been to before, places that aren't familiar and may seem downright ridiculous to you, but not to God.

First Corinthians 2:9-10 say,

> *However, as it is written: "No eye has seen, no ear has heard, no mind has conceived what God has prepared for those who love him"—but God has revealed it to us by his Spirit. The Spirit searches all things, even the deep things of God.*

You have access to things you don't know, things you've never heard of, and things you've never thought of. You have an ability past yourself to succeed in life—*through the Holy Spirit.*

My prayer is that, through this study, you'll experience victory and have your own incredible stories of being led in life by the Holy Spirit and the power of strategy!

> *No, we speak of God's secret wisdom, a wisdom that has been hidden and that God destined for our glory before time began. None of the rulers of this age understood it, for if they had, they would not have crucified the Lord of glory.*
> —1 Corinthians 2:7-8

CHAPTER 1
YOU WANT US TO DO WHAT?

STRATEGY /ˈstradəjē/ – a plan of action or policy designed to achieve a major or overall aim; the art of planning and directing overall military operations and movements in a war or battle;[1] a method or plan chosen to bring about a desired future, such as achievement of a goal or solution to a problem; the art and science of planning and marshalling resources for their most efficient and effective use.[2]

There Are No "Impossible" Situations

The God that made you knows the plan. You just need to hear it.

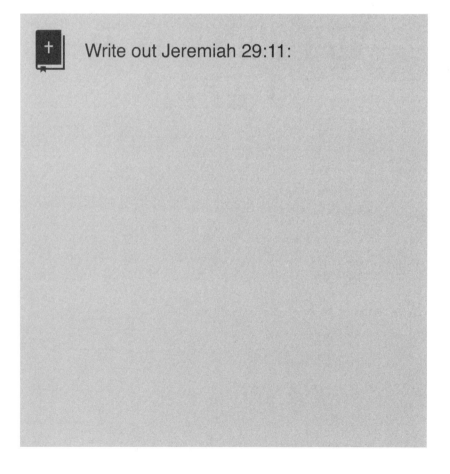

Write out Jeremiah 29:11:

Describe a time you believe you heard from the Lord, but you had no idea how to make happen what He was directing you to do, and what happened:

Describe a time that you wrestled with fear versus what the Lord was directing you to do, and what happened:

Your Financial Revolution: The Power of Strategy book is about _____ and being _____ in life by the Spirit of God.

The Holy Spirit leads people to _____ _____.

1 Google dictionary
2 www.businessdictionary.com/definition/strategy.html

KNOW THIS: EVERYTHING THAT GOD DOES IN YOUR LIFE WILL COME FROM YOUR ABILITY TO NOT ONLY KNOW HOW HIS KINGDOM OPERATES, BUT ALSO TO BE ABLE TO HEAR GOD GIVE YOU THE DIRECTION, WISDOM, AND THE ANSWERS YOU NEED.

Write out James 5:13:

Why should you pray when you have a problem?

God is able to do more than you can ever imagine when you're facing trouble. He will help you with _____, and sometimes _____, solutions and _____ so you can overcome what you feel are impossible situations.

Many times, your ability to hear the answer can be the difference between _____ and _____.

> Name one thing in your life you need God to give you direction, wisdom, or an answer about:

If you are ever going to tap into the awesome potential of the Kingdom of God, you will need to learn how to _____.

List two things you learned about how God operates from the stories in this chapter:

1. _____

2. _____

📝 Other notes from this chapter:

Strategic Pause — Change Your Mind-set

Think about the last time you were truly excited about something that was coming up in your life. Was it a party or event; a vacation; someone visiting you?

Pause and think about how the *anticipation* of that *good* thing *felt*.

That's how you should feel every day about the plans God has for your life—excited and anticipating all He has for you.

First John 5:14-15 say you should have CONFIDENCE in approaching God, knowing that if you ask anything according to His will, He hears you. And if you know that He hears you—whatever you ask—you know that you have what you ask of Him.

Work on changing your mind-set to one of anticipation of all God is going to do in your life. Start *looking forward* to the direction, wisdom, and plans He's going to download in your spirit. Choose to be a possibility-thinker rather than a problem-focuser!

"

Lord, starting today, I choose to change my mind-set to one of anticipation! I thank You that I can be confident in approaching You, knowing that if I ask anything according to Your will, You hear me, and that I have what I ask of You.

I ask that You make very clear all that I'm reading in The Power of Strategy and in Your Word, so I can continue to learn how Your Kingdom operates and have an understanding of You and Your Kingdom that I've never had before, so I can live the life You have for me.

I thank You that I hear and am led by Your Spirit! I'm more than ready for You to show me great and mighty things that only You can do!

In Jesus's Name I pray. Amen.

"

CHAPTER 2
THE KINGDOM

STRATEGY /ˈstradəjē/ – a plan of action or policy designed to achieve a major or overall aim; the art of planning and directing overall military operations and movements in a war or battle; a method or plan chosen to bring about a desired future, such as achievement of a goal or solution to a problem; the art and science of planning and marshalling resources for their most efficient and effective use.

Understanding How the Kingdom Operates

If you want to see the Holy Spirit move in your situation, you need to be clear on what the _____ says.

KNOW THIS: GOD'S KINGDOM IS JUST THAT, A KINGDOM, WHICH OPERATES WITHIN THE BOUNDARIES OF THE LAWS OF THE KINGDOM.

Jesus said to them, "Only in his hometown, among his relatives and in his own house is a prophet without honor." He could not do any miracles there, except lay his hands on a few sick people and heal them. And he was amazed at their lack of faith.

—Mark 6:4-6

Why couldn't Jesus do any miracles in his hometown?

_____

_____

The Back Story

1. Adam and Eve were placed on the earth with absolute authority over the earth realm. They were crowned with glory and honor and ruled with delegated authority from God.

2. Satan, who was already on the earth when man was created, despised man and lusted after the authority he had. Knowing he couldn't simply take Adam's crown, he had to deceive Adam into giving it to him.

3. Satan deceived Eve and Adam followed, rebelling against God and resulting in the loss of their position in God's Kingdom and putting them under the jurisdiction of Satan's kingdom.

Why did God place the Tree of the Knowledge of Good and Evil right in the middle of the Garden, next to the Tree of Life? _____

_____

_____

Man could not have been placed in the earth without a _____

_____.

**KNOW THIS: HELL WAS NEVER CREATED FOR MAN;
IT WAS CREATED FOR SATAN AND HIS DEMONS.**

God put a rescue plan in place through _____ that enables men and women to escape the judgment of hell and be brought back into the jurisdiction of His Kingdom.

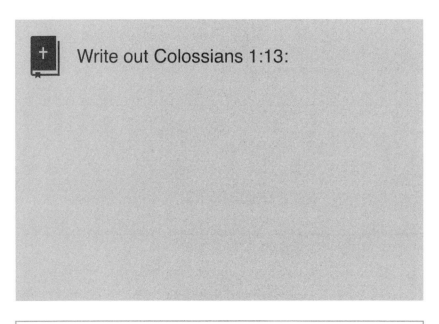

+ Write out Colossians 1:13:

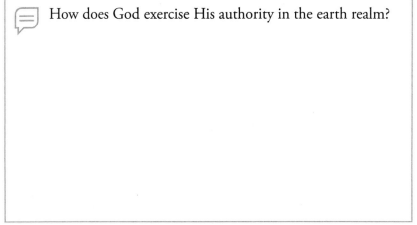

How does God exercise His authority in the earth realm?

Since men and women still have legal control of the earth (not to be confused with spiritual control), God and Satan must use _____ to get things done.

❓ Since Satan is here on the earth, he is always defending his kingdom and always trying to overtake God's plans. Because of this, God works _____ to get His plans and _____ into the earth realm.

What are two things you learned about the Kingdom from this chapter?

❓ 1. _____

_____

❓ 2. _____

_____

💬 Other notes from this chapter:

Strategic Pause — Fight Intimidation

Satan uses a lot of tactics to trick us out of our dominion. He knows that faith is the currency of the Kingdom of heaven. He knows that if your heart holds onto the Word, it's going to produce. So, he has tactics he uses to get the Word out of your heart. The Parable of the Sower in Matthew 13 tells us some of them—trouble, persecution, stirring up strife, conflict—to get you to let go of the Word. He's going to try to do something, anything, and he's going to make it *look* bigger than the Word.

Pause and consider if his tactics have been working on you.

Have you freaked out about a situation, or have you stayed in faith (agreement) with what heaven says? First Peter 5:8 tells us to be self-controlled and alert because our enemy prowls around like a roaring lion looking for someone to devour. When he sets that stage, our natural instinct is to react, to panic, to yield to fear, to let go of the Word, but God tells us not to let go, no matter what is happening. Fight back with the Word. Speak it. Put on the full armor of God so that you can stand against the devil's schemes.

"

Lord, Thank You for showing me how Your Kingdom operates, for Your Word, and for revealing the tactics the enemy uses to try to get Your Word out of my heart!

I declare Ephesians 6:11-17 over my mind and heart! I will be strong in You and Your mighty power. I put on the full armor of God so that I can take my stand against the devil's schemes. I stand firm with the belt of truth buckled around my waist, with the breastplate of righteousness in place, and with my feet fitted with the readiness that comes from the Gospel of peace. I hold the shield of faith, with which I can extinguish all the flaming arrows of the evil one. I wear my helmet of salvation and carry the sword of the Spirit, which is Your Word! I do not give in to the intimidation of the enemy! He is already defeated!

In Jesus's Name I pray. Amen.

"

CHAPTER 3
ASTONISHED

STRATEGY /'stradəjē/ – a plan of action or policy designed to achieve a major or overall aim; the art of planning and directing overall military operations and movements in a war or battle; a method or plan chosen to bring about a desired future, such as achievement of a goal or solution to a problem; the art and science of planning and marshalling resources for their most efficient and effective use.

God Wants to Use You to Demonstrate His Kingdom

The world is hungry to see the real thing, and God loves to amaze the world.

God wants to surprise you with supernatural plans and strategies that will bring evidence of His reality and love to those around you.

The Kingdom of God	The kingdom of darkness/ earth curse system
• whole • always more than enough • overflowing nets on first catch • provision and rest • life, and life more abundantly	• broken • impoverished • fish all night and catch nothing • painful toil and sweat • survival

KNOW THIS: IF YOU CAN'T TEACH SOMETHING, YOU CAN'T LIVE IT. IF YOU DON'T KNOW HOW THE CATCH SHOWED UP IN LUKE 5, YOU'LL NEVER BE ABLE TO DUPLICATE IT.

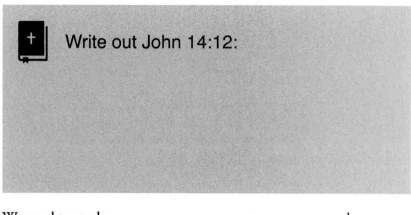

Write out John 14:12:

We need to study _____ so that we can determine what hinders or what facilitates the free flow of the Holy Spirit in any situation.

The huge catch of fish in Luke 5 was a result of a supernatural plan and strategy given by the _____ to Peter through Jesus that day. It was secret _____.

KNOW THIS: THE SAME HOLY SPIRIT THAT TOLD JESUS THAT DAY, IN LUKE 5, WHERE THE FISH WERE IS HERE TODAY AND LIVES IN YOU IF YOU'RE A BELIEVER!

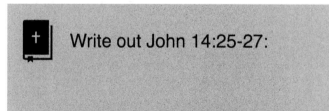

Write out John 14:25-27:

What was Jesus's peace and why?

According to *Strong's Exhaustive Concordance of the Bible* (3875), the Greek word translated counselor means:

☐ One summoned, or called to one's side, especially called to one's _____.

☐ One who pleads another's cause before a judge.

☐ A counsel for _____.

☐ A legal assistant, or an _____.

☐ _____ or one bringing aid.

In what areas of your life do you believe you easily follow the direction of the Holy Spirit?

In what areas of your life do you recognize you struggle to follow the direction of the Holy Spirit?

You Have a Part to Play

God has given you the Holy Spirit to help you with the answers you need in life, but you have your part to play, working _____ the Holy Spirit to bring God's will to pass.

In what ways do you recognize that you've been "fishing in your own ability" and coming up empty, or close to it?

What is a "mailbox mentality"?

KNOW THIS: YOU NEED TO HAVE A MIND-SET OF LOOKING FOR OPPORTUNITY. YOU HAVE TO HARVEST, OR CAPTURE, WEALTH IN THE EARTH REALM. GOD WORKS WITH US TO BRING US TO AN INTERSECTION OF OPPORTUNITY (CLUE: LOOK FOR A PROBLEM TO SOLVE) AND THEN GIVES US A PLAN TO CAPTURE IT.

What are two things you took from the testimonies shared in this chapter?

1. _____

_____

2. _____

_____

Other notes from this chapter:

Strategic Pause — Rise to the Challenge

Do you love a good challenge, or would you rather steer clear of them?

Here's the thing: God wants to get a lot more done than you can even think of. He wants more impact in the earth realm. He's waiting for people who will rise to the challenge. He's waiting for YOU.

God has designed you to have a part to play, working with the Holy Spirit to bring His will to pass. He has bigger plans for you than you have for yourself!

Pause and consider if you've been willing to embrace them.

Does that make you uncomfortable? If it does, good! Because you can't do it by yourself! You need God! He wants to pull you out into the deep water, where you must rely on Him or you'll sink! Just remember, all things are possible for those that believe (Mark 9:23), and rise to the challenge!

Lord, I thank You that You have given me the Holy Spirit to help me with the answers I need in life. Help me not to try to "fish" in my own strength but to rely solely on You! Give me the strength and the courage to rise to the challenges You have for me, so I can do my part as I work with the Holy Spirit to bring Your will to pass in the earth!

In Jesus's Name I pray. Amen.

CHAPTER 4
DON'T LEAVE HOME WITHOUT THIS.

STRATEGY /'stradəjē/ – a plan of action or policy designed to achieve a major or overall aim; the art of planning and directing overall military operations and movements in a war or battle; a method or plan chosen to bring about a desired future, such as achievement of a goal or solution to a problem; the art and science of planning and marshalling resources for their most efficient and effective use.

Reviewing the Basics

If you're going to lead a life full of Holy Spirit strategies and Holy Spirit-led victories, first, you need to be _____, and then, second, you need to be _____ _____.

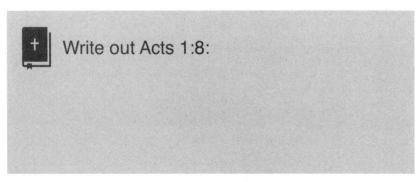

Write out Acts 1:4-5:

Write out Acts 1:8:

The Baptism of the Holy Spirit is for _____, and the _____ of God is available today just as it was when Jesus walked the earth. The best part is that it's for _____ believers—it's for anyone who asks!

The word "anointing" means to _____.

KNOW THIS: IT WAS ONLY AFTER JESUS RECEIVED THE ANOINTING OF THE HOLY SPIRIT THAT HE WAS ABLE TO DO THE WORKS OF THE KINGDOM. IF JESUS NEEDED THE ANOINTING, SO DO WE! YOU NEED THE POWER OF THE HOLY SPIRIT TO GET THINGS DONE!

The Bible says you will receive power when the Holy Spirit comes _____ you, not _____ you.

Being born again and being baptized by the Holy Spirit are two different events.

Summarize Mark 16:17-18 in your own words:

How has this chapter changed what you believe about the Baptism of the Holy Spirit and speaking in tongues?

Other notes from this chapter:

Strategic Pause — Posture Yourself

It's never God's intention that you try to do life by yourself. He has a plan. You just need to posture yourself so that you can receive the anointing.

In Judges 6 and 7, we read the story of Gideon. Gideon had some issues to work through—and some altars to tear down that were holding him back. He was obedient to God, and the Spirit of the Lord came upon him.

Pause and ask God to reveal any areas of your life that *you* need to get right.

Are there any altars holding you back that you need to tear down? Do you need to get your heart right? Do you need to get your family right? Do you need to get your marriage right? What do you need to change so that, when you face the battle, the anointing of God will come upon you and give you the plan for your victory? Get it right and get postured for God to use you and to be a success.

"

Lord, I thank You that You already have the plan for my victory. Open my eyes and reveal to me exactly what I need to get right in my life—any altars I need to tear down that are keeping me from being postured to receive all You have for me—and help me to tear them down swiftly and permanently!

In Jesus's Name I pray. Amen.

"

CHAPTER 5
SCRIPTURAL EVIDENCE

STRATEGY /ˈstradəjē/ – a plan of action or policy designed to achieve a major or overall aim; the art of planning and directing overall military operations and movements in a war or battle; a method or plan chosen to bring about a desired future, such as achievement of a goal or solution to a problem; the art and science of planning and marshalling resources for their most efficient and effective use.

Understanding the Baptism of the Holy Spirit

When the day of Pentecost came, they were all together in one place. Suddenly a sound like the blowing of a violent wind came from heaven and filled the whole house where they were sitting. They saw what seemed to be tongues of fire that separated and came to rest on each of them. _____ were filled with the Holy Spirit and began to _____ as the _____.

Now there were staying in Jerusalem God-fearing Jews from every nation under heaven. When they heard this sound, a crowd came together in bewilderment, because each one heard them speaking in his own language.

Utterly amazed, they asked: "Are not all these men who are speaking Galileans? Then how is it that each of us hears them in his own native language? Parthians, Medes and Elamites; residents of Mesopotamia, Judea and Cappadocia, Pontus and Asia, Phrygia and Pamphylia, Egypt and the parts of Libya near Cyrene; visitors from Rome (both Jews and converts to Judaism); Cretans and Arabs—we hear them declaring the wonders of God in our own tongues!"

Amazed and perplexed, they asked one another, "What does this mean?" Some, however, made fun of them and said, "They have had too much wine."

—Acts 2:1-13

Tongues weren't used to preach the Gospel then, and they're not used to preach the Gospel now.

When people see the signs, when they see the _____ _____ of the Kingdom, they're going to pay close attention to what you say.

When the apostles in Jerusalem heard that Samaria had accepted the word of God, they sent Peter and John to Samaria. When they arrived, they prayed for them that they might receive the Holy Spirit, because the Holy Spirit had not yet _____ any of them; they had simply been baptized into the name of the Lord Jesus. Then Peter and John placed their hands on them, and they received the Holy Spirit.

—Acts 8:14-17

 Write out 1 Corinthians 14:18:

What is the significance of what Paul says in Acts 19:1-2?

The Baptism of the Holy Spirit is controversial in churches not because it's not in the Bible, but because _____ _____.

The Baptism of the Holy Spirit gives you a _____ _____—God's power—to do the _____ so God is glorified!

Other notes from this chapter:

Strategic Pause — Bring God on the Scene

God wants everyone healthy. He wants everyone whole. He wants to destroy the darkness in the earth. He wants to set things right. He wants vengeance for what's happened to His creation. He wants to release righteousness into the earth. But He can't do this sitting up in heaven. So He figured out a way to get on the scene—the Baptism of the Holy Spirit. But WE have to be willing to let Him use us.

Isaiah 61:1-2 give us a better understanding of how He wants to use us:

> *The Spirit of the Sovereign Lord is on me, because the Lord has anointed me to preach good news to the poor. He has sent me to bind up the brokenhearted, to proclaim freedom for the captives and release from darkness for the prisoners, to proclaim the year of the Lord's favor and the day of vengeance of our God, to comfort all who mourn.*

Pause and consider whether or not you've been allowing God to use you.

Or have you been more like a person who has a superhero suit but is letting it collect dust on a shelf or keeping it buried in the back of a closet?

Make sure you're bringing God on the scene, using the power God has given you, not letting it go to waste.

"

Lord, I thank You that You want to bring restoration back to the earth, and that You have given me Your Spirit to guide me! Help me to be a witness for You in the earth by proclaiming the Good News to the poor, binding up the brokenhearted, proclaiming freedom for the captives, releasing prisoners from darkness, and comforting all who mourn!

In Jesus's Name I pray. Amen

"

CHAPTER 6
DO ALL PRAY IN TONGUES?

STRATEGY /ˈstradəjē/ – a plan of action or policy designed to achieve a major or overall aim; the art of planning and directing overall military operations and movements in a war or battle; a method or plan chosen to bring about a desired future, such as achievement of a goal or solution to a problem; the art and science of planning and marshalling resources for their most efficient and effective use.

Don't Be Misled

In the church service itself, some people will operate in the gift of tongues and interpretation, as recorded in 1 Corinthians 12, but all will not or should not operate in that gift for the purpose of _____ the whole body.

When Paul says all do not speak in tongues, he is referring to_____ _____.

KNOW THIS: EVERY BELIEVER WILL HAVE THE ABILITY TO PRAY IN TONGUES, BUT NOT EVERYONE WILL HAVE THAT UNCTION TO STEP OUT INTO THE GIFT OF TONGUES AND INTERPRETATION IN A CHURCH SERVICE.

Write out 1 Corinthians 14:13:

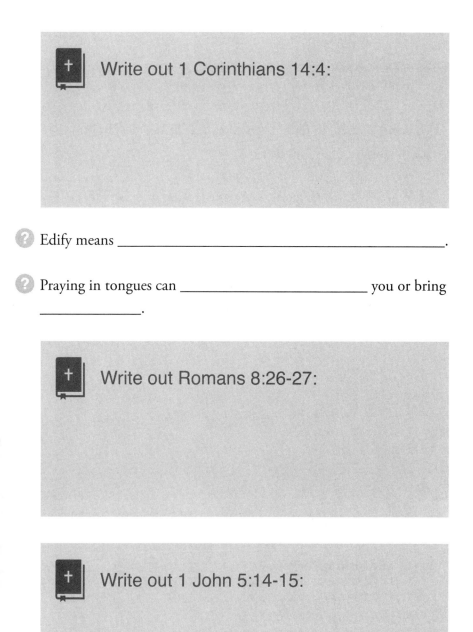

Write out 1 Corinthians 14:4:

Edify means _____.

Praying in tongues can _____ you or bring
_____.

Write out Romans 8:26-27:

Write out 1 John 5:14-15:

(?) Without knowing or being confident of the will of God, you can't
_____ (being in
agreement with God).

(?) If you can't operate in faith, then you won't be able to tap into the
grace or the _____ of God.

> What is our weakness?

(?) Without knowing _____, you can't know and
believe that you _____ from God when you pray.

(?) You tap into hearing the Spirit by _____
_____.

(?) The Spirit of God prays the perfect will of God for each situation
through your own spirit when you _____
_____.

Summarize 1 Corinthians 2:9-13 in your own words:

According to 1 Thessalonians 5:23, we are three parts: _____, _____, and _____.

Your _____ is the God part of you; your _____ is your mind, will, and emotions; and your body is your body.

Write out 1 Corinthians 14:14-15:

❓ *For anyone who speaks in a tongue does not speak to men but to God. Indeed, no one understands him;* _____

_____.

—1 Corinthians 14:2

💬 What is "revelation"?

❓ First Corinthians 2:16 says you have _____

_____.

❓ You have the ability, by praying in the Spirit (tongues), to receive _____, things you didn't know; and by that knowledge, you're able to make right judgments or decisions about _____ things!

❓ The Baptism of the Holy Spirit is God's _____ _____—how He can download His will into the earth realm without the devil knowing what is going on.

Praying in the Spirit:

- Is part of your spiritual _____ (Ephesians 6:18).

- Allows you to pick up on _____ that will help you sidestep the enemy, or advance with unique and unusual tactics.

- Helps you make the right _____ in life by tapping into the mind of Christ.

Write out 1 Thessalonians 5:17:

Other notes from this chapter:

Strategic Pause — Pray Big

The Lord's Prayer in Matthew 6 isn't just a saying to hang on a wall. It also wasn't necessarily meant to teach you the exact words you should pray. Jesus was teaching us *how* to pray.

Pause and take a look at Matthew 6:9-13 in your Bible.

Then, when you pray:

→ Approach God as your Father, which means you have access to what He has.

→ Acknowledge He is great, awesome, holy, and revered.

→ Be confident that God has given you the authority to help bring His Kingdom into the earth.

→ Trust that you have permission to approach God and ask Him for what you need.

→ Forgive and have His heart toward others.

→ Receive revelation concerning what the enemy is setting up for your destruction.

Lord, I praise You! Great is Your Name! Thank You so much for sending Jesus to take the place of my sins so that I can be called Your child and have full access to the rights and benefits of Your estate as a co-heir with Him. I will walk in the authority You have given me as a citizen of Your great Kingdom, bringing Your will into the earth realm. I praise You that I can come to You with all of my needs and trust that You will come through. I pray that You forgive me of my sins and show me anyone that I need to forgive. Help me to keep my heart soft toward both You and others. I trust You fully to help me and warn me of the tactics of the enemy in my life, and to lead me in life every day in all things.

In Jesus's Name I pray. Amen.

CHAPTER 7
THE TREASURE CHEST

STRATEGY /ˈstradəjē/ – a plan of action or policy designed to achieve a major or overall aim; the art of planning and directing overall military operations and movements in a war or battle; a method or plan chosen to bring about a desired future, such as achievement of a goal or solution to a problem; the art and science of planning and marshalling resources for their most efficient and effective use.

The Holy Spirit Has the Plan

What is one area of your life, or situation you're facing, that you really need God to give you direction about?

The Kingdom operates by _____, not favors. God doesn't play favorites.

In what ways do you recognize that you *haven't* been acting like a member of God's household or a citizen of His Kingdom with access to all that He has?

Thus says the Lord, your Redeemer, The Holy One of Israel: "I am the Lord your God, Who _____, *Who* _____."

—Isaiah 48:17 (NKJV)

The Holy Spirit has YOUR plan.

There is nothing more powerful than having the _____. Without the plan, the picture is a dream. But with the plan, the dream can be _____.

KNOW THIS: GOD CAN GIVE YOU THE PLAN, BUT YOU HAVE TO DO YOUR PART IN THE PLAN FOR IT TO WORK OUT. IT'S YOU AND GOD!

Write out Matthew 13:44:

 The kingdom of God does not come with your careful observation, nor will people say, "Here it is," or "There it is," because the kingdom of God is _____."

—Luke 17:20-21

 Write out Ephesians 3:20:

 Typically, when we need something or need help, we've trained ourselves to look _____ of ourselves for the answer. But now, the Holy Spirit, God Himself, lives _____ us and is our help.

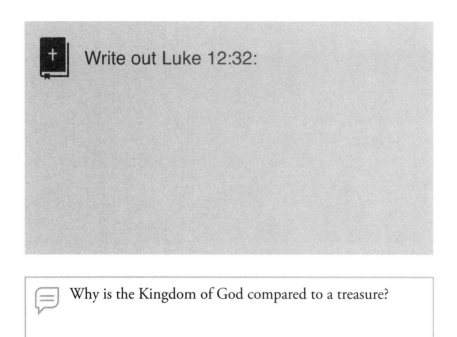

Write out Luke 12:32:

Why is the Kingdom of God compared to a treasure?

When we think of treasure, we usually think of things like gold and silver, but in reality, treasure is really what we need in the moment—an answer, direction, an idea, etc.

God's secrets are hidden _____ you, not _____ you. Satan dwells in darkness and doesn't know the plans of God.

The disciples came to him and asked, "Why do you speak to the people in parables?"

He replied, "The knowledge of the secrets [these things that are hidden] of the kingdom of heaven _____, but not to them."

— Matthew 13:10-11

 Write out Isaiah 45:3:

The Bible says Satan will _____ if he can pick up on what God is doing.

No, we speak of God's secret wisdom, a wisdom that has been hidden and that God destined for our glory before time began. None of the rulers of this age understood it, for if they had, they would not have crucified the Lord of glory.

— 1 Corinthians 2:7-8

God is never _____. What you see as a delay is working for you by keeping the answer hidden until it's time for it to be revealed.

KNOW THIS: BECAUSE GOD IS ALWAYS MOVING UNDERCOVER UNTIL THE MOMENT OF VICTORY, YOU NEED TO REMEMBER THAT GOD'S PLANS ARE ALWAYS SPECIFIC IN LOCATION, METHOD, TIMING, AND OPERATIONAL DETAIL.

Why is it important that you don't always act right away on the idea, direction, or plan God gives you?

Once you hear the idea or direction, you must not move on it until you have _____.

Many times, the Holy Spirit will reveal an idea to us, not revealing it for us to move on the idea at that moment but to allow us to _____ so that we can actually _____ _____.

The _____ phase is the most important part of the process.

Describe a time you *didn't* properly prepare to capture an opportunity and what happened:

Describe a time you *did* properly prepare to capture an opportunity and what happened:

_____ and _____ are just as important, or more important, than the idea itself!

Declare this version of Matthew 13:44 over yourself and your life:

> *The Kingdom of heaven in me gives me the knowledge or access to the knowledge of the secrets, or hidden things that God knows. This knowledge is accessible from the Spirit of God, Himself that is within ME. When I find or hear that secret knowledge that is a treasure to me, an answer for my life, I hide it again in my heart and mind. Then, with joy, I go with all my strength to pursue, with careful preparation, the direction and instruction revealed to me, taking hold of and capturing my answers!*

Other notes from this chapter:

Strategic Pause — Seize Opportunities
God knows where things are. He knows where your provision is. The Holy Spirit will give you new direction, new ideas, and new concepts by revelation.

Carry a notepad and a pen with you. Keep paper and pens next to your bed.

Pause to write down *every* idea and concept, no matter how silly they might seem.

Most people filter opportunities and ideas through what they perceive their ability to be. This means most people discard ideas by the dozens because they don't think they can do them. But God isn't limited to what you know how to do. The ideas He gives you might seem so weird to you that you can't process them fully. Write them down so you have time to think about them.

"

Lord, I thank You that You know where my provision is and that You give me new direction, new ideas, and new concepts by revelation! I excitedly anticipate the opportunities You're sending my way! Help me not to miss any of them!

In Jesus's Name I pray. Amen.

"

CHAPTER 8
THE HARD PLACE OF PROMOTION

STRATEGY /ˈstradəjē/ – a plan of action or policy designed to achieve a major or overall aim; the art of planning and directing overall military operations and movements in a war or battle; a method or plan chosen to bring about a desired future, such as achievement of a goal or solution to a problem; the art and science of planning and marshalling resources for their most efficient and effective use.

Don't Shy Away from the Hard Things

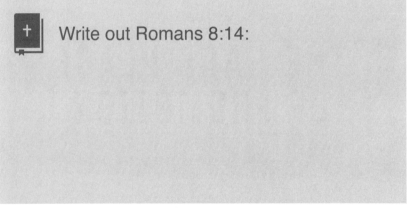

Write out Romans 8:14:

Summarize the story of Daniel hearing from the Lord in Daniel 2 in your own words:

What was the result of Daniel being able to hear God's voice?

KNOW THIS: THE WORLD WILL PAY BIG MONEY TO PEOPLE WHO CAN SOLVE BIG PROBLEMS!

It is the hard place that gives you the perfect opportunity to bring the _____.

The hard place is the perfect setup for your next _____ _____!

Don't be afraid to step out into hard places for fear of making a mistake. The Holy Spirit is able to warn you of a potential mistake if you listen to Him.

Write out Matthew 14:27:

The hard and impossible places are not hard and impossible when

_____!

Other notes from this chapter:

Strategic Pause — Look for Problems
As you begin to allow the Holy Spirit to lead you, you'll find that
He leads you by providing you with solutions to problems that are
around you. By recognizing and finding solutions to life's problems,
you will be postured for promotion or propelled to new places of
responsibility, but it will require change on your part. This might

mean that you find yourself thrust into a tense situation, like David was with Goliath.

Pause and tell yourself that pressure and problems are actually opportunities in disguise.

God is with you! Train yourself to look at problems as opportunities! It will be a key to your victory!

Lord, I consider it pure joy whenever I face trials, because I know that the testing of my faith produces perseverance. Let perseverance finish its work so that I may be mature and complete, not lacking anything (James 1:2-4). I thank You that I don't shy away from the hard things because You are with me and give me the answers. I praise You for the opportunities You are sending my way and the promotion and wealth that are behind them!

In Jesus's Name I pray. Amen.

CHAPTER 9
THE STILL, SMALL VOICE

STRATEGY /ˈstradəjē/ – a plan of action or policy designed to achieve a major or overall aim; the art of planning and directing overall military operations and movements in a war or battle; a method or plan chosen to bring about a desired future, such as achievement of a goal or solution to a problem; the art and science of planning and marshalling resources for their most efficient and effective use.

Hearing God's Voice

Do you believe you've heard the voice of God? If yes, share an example. If no, why do you think you haven't?

The normal voice of the Holy Spirit is _____ _____.

The conscience is:

- (?) • An _____ of right and wrong.

- (?) • _____
  within each person.

- (?) • What speaks on our behalf (_____)
  or condemns (_____) us.

- (?) • An _____ of the Creator and His
  requirements to live the lives we were created to live.

(?) No one can _____
their conscience, but if a person continues to _____
the voice of their conscience, that voice will get quieter and quieter.

(?) Paul warns that ignoring your conscience can _____
_____.

KNOW THIS: IF YOU OVERRIDE YOUR CONSCIENCE, YOU'LL HARDEN YOUR HEART; AND IT WILL BECOME EASIER AND EASIER TO DO, UNTIL YOU CAN'T HEAR GOD AT ALL.

> Have you ever overridden your conscience? Why or why not?

If you want to hear God, you need to:

1. Keep your conscience _____.

2. Be quick to _____.

Other notes from this chapter:

Strategic Pause — Test Your Thoughts

Did you know the Bible says we can deceive ourselves? How? With our *thoughts*.

See, thoughts are seeds. They're pictures. What you listen to, what you look at, the things you do, the friends you hang around, all produce thoughts—pictures—in your mind. When you begin to concentrate on those pictures, they produce desire, for good or for bad, and your heart can't tell the difference.

Pause and ask yourself, and the Holy Spirit, how your thoughts measure against what God says. And wait for Him to answer.

Make changes if you need to. Start umpiring your thoughts. If they don't line up with what God says, replace them immediately with right thoughts—from the Word. Test your thoughts. Elevate God's Word above all of the other voices in your life, and set your heart on it.

Lord, I thank You that I can hear Your voice and that You have given me the Holy Spirit to help me test my thoughts! I demolish arguments and every pretension that sets itself up against the knowledge of God, and I take captive every thought to make it obedient to Christ (2 Corinthians 10:5).

In Jesus's Name I pray. Amen.

CHAPTER 10
VISIONS AND DREAMS

STRATEGY /ˈstradəjē/ – a plan of action or policy designed to achieve a major or overall aim; the art of planning and directing overall military operations and movements in a war or battle; a method or plan chosen to bring about a desired future, such as achievement of a goal or solution to a problem; the art and science of planning and marshalling resources for their most efficient and effective use.

Other Ways the Holy Spirit Speaks to You

> *And afterward, I will pour out my Spirit on all people. Your sons and daughters will prophesy, your old men will dream dreams, your young men will see visions. Even on my servants, both men and women, I will pour out my Spirit in those days.*
> —Joel 2:28-29

_____ and _____ are a very big part of how the Holy Spirit speaks to us. Dreams are pictures we see when we're _____, and visions are pictures we see when we're _____.

Have you ever experienced a dream or vision from the Holy Spirit? If so, share one here. If not, why do you think you haven't?

Dreams are the _____ of the Holy Spirit.

KNOW THIS: GOD WILL ONLY LEAD YOU WITH PARTIAL DREAMS AND VISIONS OF YOUR FUTURE, JUST ENOUGH TO KEEP YOU MOVING IN THE RIGHT DIRECTION UNTIL YOU'RE MATURE ENOUGH TO OCCUPY HIS PLAN.

You have to _____ dreams.

Dreams and visions can be used by God to:
- Send you a message.
- Give you a picture of your future.
- Give you direction or instruction.
- Communicate the plan of God.
- Change your life.
- Warn you.
- Give you strategy.
- Comfort you.

One more method that God uses to help direct strategy is

_____ .

 Write out 1 Corinthians 14:3:

According to Paul, prophecy is only to _____ direction, not to _____ direction.

KNOW THIS: ONCE YOU ARE BORN AGAIN, THE HOLY SPIRIT ON THE INSIDE OF YOU WILL BE THE ONE THAT TELLS YOU WHAT TO DO. YOU DON'T NEED A MAN OR A WOMAN TO TELL YOU WHAT YOU'RE CALLED TO DO FOR JESUS. BUT A WORD OF PROPHECY CAN CONFIRM SOMETHING THAT YOU ALREADY KNOW.

Other notes from this chapter:

Strategic Pause — Dream Again

As children, we pretend to be superheroes, famous people, and great leaders; we think we can do anything. Then life happens, and our once-crystal-clear, totally doable goals and achievable dreams turn into out-of-reach impossibilities.

No matter what twists and turns your life has taken, you are STILL destined by God to do great things.

Pause and make today the day you clear the cobwebs and get out of the lull.

It's time for you to dream again.

You may have no clue how it might happen, but you don't need to know. Remember Abraham? In Genesis 15, we read that he wanted an heir. He and his wife, Sarah, wanted a child. They had a dream, a desire. But as the years went by, and Abraham and Sarah got much older, and *well* past childbearing years, their dream no longer seemed possible.

Sarah knew it was impossible for her to conceive, but she didn't have to figure it out. She just had to know that God would make it possible. After all, it was His promise, His glory, and His goodness that assured her that He had the power and intent to bring her dream to pass. She just had to put her confidence in Him.

The same went for Abraham. He may have known that his wife's womb was as good as dead as far as conceiving was concerned, but he only needed to be convinced that God had the power to do what He said.

Just like Abraham and Sarah, or Drenda and me, you can see your dreams birthed in your own life as you believe God's Word and His promises.

"

Lord, I thank You for showing me the future You have planned for me through dreams and visions. I praise You for giving me dreams that motivate me to get out of bed in the morning— dreams that allow me to follow my passions, use my talents, make a difference in the world, and win in life. I know it doesn't matter if I have no ability in myself to see my dreams come to pass, because You make a way when there seems to be no way, and You have the power to do what You say!

In Jesus's Name I pray. Amen.

"

CHAPTER 11
THE HOLY SPIRIT SOUNDS LIKE MY BOSS.

STRATEGY /ˈstradəjē/ – a plan of action or policy designed to achieve a major or overall aim; the art of planning and directing overall military operations and movements in a war or battle; a method or plan chosen to bring about a desired future, such as achievement of a goal or solution to a problem; the art and science of planning and marshalling resources for their most efficient and effective use.

Are You Hindering Your Ability to Hear the Holy Spirit?

You can only walk with authority as you are _____ _____.

> In what ways can you confirm you *are* submitted to the authorities God has placed in your life?

> In what areas might you need to work on respecting and submitting to the authorities God has placed in your life?

Declare this version of Luke 16:10-12:

> I can be trusted with very little, so I can also be trusted with much. I am trustworthy in handling worldly wealth, so I will be trusted with true riches. I am trustworthy with the property of others as well as my own.

How do you know if you can be trusted with authority?

Why was Saul disqualified as king?

What does it mean to be "after God's heart"?

Being obedient is spiritual _____.

There is no such thing as an insignificant job. There are no small assignments.

KNOW THIS: IF YOU CAN'T SUBMIT TO A PERSON THAT YOU CAN SEE, YOU WON'T SUBMIT TO GOD, WHO YOU DON'T SEE.

Everyone must pass the _____ test.

_____ is better than sacrifice.

Learning to respect and honor authority starts _____

_____.

> What does the condition of your possessions right now say about your personal responsibility? What might the condition of your car or house convey to a prospective employer?

God is your promoter, but He doesn't promote on _____ _____ alone. Your _____ has to be tested as well.

KNOW THIS: GOD SOUNDS LIKE YOUR BOSS BECAUSE YOUR BOSS IS AN INSTRUMENT USED BY GOD TO TRAIN YOU FOR YOUR NEXT ASSIGNMENT AND TO HOLD YOU TO SUBMISSION.

Slaves, obey your earthly masters with respect and fear, and with sincerity of heart, just as you would obey Christ. _____ not only to win their favor when their eye is on you, but as slaves of Christ, doing the will of God from your heart. _____, as if you were serving the Lord, not men, because you know that the Lord will reward everyone for whatever good he does, whether he is slave or free.

And masters, treat your slaves in the same way. Do not threaten them, since you know that he who is both their Master and yours is in heaven, and there is no favoritism with him.

—Ephesians 6:5-9

Other notes from this chapter:

Strategic Pause — Pass the Test

God will lead you through the authorities in your life, but you won't be able to receive from anyone you don't honor. That's why the enemy is ALWAYS trying to tear down authorities and why our culture is disintegrating in the areas of honor, authority, and integrity.

We've all been there—out to lunch when someone was talking about the boss, or with a friend who managed to get out of a speeding ticket, or at the grocery store when a kid talked back to her parent. But what did you think when it happened? Did you just shrug it off as normal? Or did your spirit throw up a caution flag?

See, the culture tells us that *we* get to judge whether or not a person is worthy of honor and respect, but the Bible says there is no authority except that which *God* has established (Romans 13:1). That means we are to honor and respect those in authority whether we like them or not and whether we agree with them or not. We don't get to judge or choose.

No example shows us this better than that of David and Saul. Remember that Saul wanted David dead. Yet we read that when David had an opportunity to kill Saul, he was conscience-stricken. Yes, he knew that Saul was trying to kill him, but he also knew that Saul was God's anointed. He still respected the *position* and the authority. David knew it was not *his* place to deal with Saul—it was *God's* place.

How you relate to the authorities God has placed over you speaks volumes about your character and your future. First Timothy 2:1-2 tell us to pray for those in authority, that we may live peaceful and quiet lives in all godliness and holiness.

Don't help Satan discredit any authorities in your life. Give them the honor and respect that is due them, not because of who they are but because you love God and want to honor Him.

Pause and pray for those that have authority over you.

Leadership is a lot harder than you think it is. Realize that as you humble yourself and submit to the authorities in your life, you are passing an important test.

"

Lord, I thank You that _____ will seek You first. I ask You to give them a desire to know and trust You. I ask You to teach them the truth of Your commands and that he/she will want to trust and obey You, Father, above all else. May _____ seek Your will before making decisions, especially when they're making decisions that influence and affect others. Please guide and direct him/her; and by the power of Your Spirit, be a shield of protection around them, and keep them safe from temptation and evil.

In Jesus's Name I pray. Amen.

"

ANSWER KEY

Chapter 1

Your Financial Revolution: The Power of Strategy book is about <u>hearing</u> and being <u>led</u> in life by the Spirit of God.

The Holy Spirit leads people to <u>do greater things than they ever dreamed possible</u>.

Why should you pray when you have a problem? <u>Because you need to hear answers, direction, and the solution</u>.

God is able to do more than you can ever imagine when you're facing trouble. He will help you with <u>unique</u>, and sometimes <u>strange</u>, solutions and <u>strategies</u> so you can overcome what you feel are impossible situations.

Many times, your ability to hear the answer can be the difference between <u>life</u> and <u>death</u>.

If you are ever going to tap into the awesome potential of the Kingdom of God, you will need to learn how to <u>hear the Holy Spirit</u>.

Chapter 2

If you want to see the Holy Spirit move in your situation, you need to be clear on what the <u>law</u> says.

Why couldn't Jesus do any miracles in his hometown? <u>The people's lack of faith</u>.

Why did God place the Tree of the Knowledge of Good and Evil right in the middle of the Garden, next to the Tree of Life? <u>To make it legal for Him to invade Satan's territory, God had to give man a choice to serve Him or Satan</u>.

Man could not have been placed in the earth without a <u>free will</u>.

God put a rescue plan in place through <u>Jesus Christ</u> that enables men and women to escape the judgment of hell and be brought back into the jurisdiction of His Kingdom.

How does God exercise His authority in the earth realm? <u>By finding a man or woman who believes Him and is totally persuaded of heaven's authority</u>.

Since men and women still have legal control of the earth (not to be confused with spiritual control), God and Satan must use <u>people</u> to get things done.

Since Satan is here on the earth, he is always defending his kingdom and always trying to overtake God's plans. Because of this, God works <u>undercover</u> to get His plans and <u>strategies</u> into the earth realm.

Chapter 3

We need to study the laws of the Kingdom so that we can determine what hinders or what facilitates the free flow of the Holy Spirit in any situation.

The huge catch of fish in Luke 5 was a result of a supernatural plan and strategy given by the Holy Spirit to Peter through Jesus that day. It was secret knowledge.

What was Jesus's peace and why? The Holy Spirit who told Him how to handle every situation that He encountered.

According to *Strong's Exhaustive Concordance of the Bible* (3875), the Greek word translated counselor means:

- One summoned, or called to one's side, especially called to one's aid.
- One who pleads another's cause before a judge.
- A counsel for defense.
- A legal assistant, or an advocate.
- Helper or one bringing aid.

God has given you the Holy Spirit to help you with the answers you need in life, but you have your part to play, working with the Holy Spirit to bring God's will to pass.

What is a "mailbox mentality"? Simply thinking that God is going to take care of the problem, putting the money in your mailbox without it requiring anything of, or any work from, you

Chapter 4

If you're going to lead a life full of Holy Spirit strategies and Holy Spirit-led victories, first, you need to be <u>born again</u>, and then, second, you need to be <u>baptized in the Holy Spirit</u>.

The Baptism of the Holy Spirit is for <u>today</u>, and the <u>power</u> of God is available today just as it was when Jesus walked the earth. The best part is that it's for <u>all</u> believers—it's for anyone who asks!

The word "anointing" means to <u>apply to</u>.

The Bible says you will receive power when the Holy Spirit comes <u>ON</u> you, not <u>IN</u> you.

Chapter 5

When the day of Pentecost came, they were all together in one place. Suddenly a sound like the blowing of a violent wind came from heaven and filled the whole house where they were sitting. They saw what seemed to be tongues of fire that separated and came to rest on each of them. <u>All of them</u> were filled with the Holy Spirit and began to <u>speak in other tongues</u> as the <u>Spirit enabled them</u>.

Now there were staying in Jerusalem God-fearing Jews from every nation under heaven. When they heard this sound, a crowd came together in bewilderment, because each one heard them speaking in his own language.

Utterly amazed, they asked: "Are not all these men who are speaking Galileans? Then how is it that each of us hears them in his own native language? Parthians, Medes and Elamites; residents of Mesopotamia, Judea and Cappadocia, Pontus and Asia, Phrygia and Pamphylia, Egypt and the parts of Libya near Cyrene; visitors from Rome (both Jews and converts to Judaism); Cretans and Arabs—we hear them declaring the wonders of God in our own tongues!"

Amazed and perplexed, they asked one another, "What does this mean?" Some, however, made fun of them and said, "They have had too much wine."

—Acts 2:1-13

When people see the signs, when they see the <u>evidence</u> of the Kingdom, they're going to pay close attention to what you say.

> *When the apostles in Jerusalem heard that Samaria had accepted the word of God, they sent Peter and John to Samaria. When they arrived, they prayed for them that they might receive the Holy Spirit, because the Holy Spirit had not yet <u>come upon</u> any of them; they had simply been baptized into the name of the Lord Jesus. Then Peter and John placed their hands on them, and they received the Holy Spirit.*
>
> —Acts 8:14-17

What is the significance of what Paul says in Acts 19:1-2? <u>Whether or not they were baptized in the Holy Spirit was Paul's first concern when he came across the believers. He also realized that being born again was not the same as being baptized in the Holy Spirit. He was saying, "Don't leave home without it!"</u>

The Baptism of the Holy Spirit is controversial in churches not because it's not in the Bible, but because <u>the devil hates it so much</u>.

The Baptism of the Holy Spirit gives you a <u>reservoir of power</u>— God's power—to do the <u>works of Jesus</u> so God is glorified!

Chapter 6

In the church service itself, some people will operate in the gift of tongues and interpretation, as recorded in 1 Corinthians 12, but all will not or should not operate in that gift for the purpose of <u>edifying</u> the whole body.

When Paul says all do not speak in tongues, he is referring to <u>in the church or the church gathering</u>.

Edify means <u>to instruct or benefit, especially morally or spiritually, to uplift</u>.

Praying in tongues can <u>edify</u> you or bring <u>instruction</u>.

Without knowing or being confident of the will of God, you can't <u>operate in faith</u> (being in agreement with God).

If you can't operate in faith, then you won't be able to tap into the grace or the <u>power</u> of God.

What is our weakness? <u>That we don't know how to pray</u>.

Without knowing <u>the will of God</u>, you can't know and believe that you <u>receive</u> from God when you pray.

You tap into hearing the Spirit by <u>praying in the Spirit, or in tongues</u>.

The Spirit of God prays the perfect will of God for each situation, through your own spirit, when you <u>pray in tongues</u>.

According to 1 Thessalonians 5:23, we are three parts: <u>spirit, soul,</u> and <u>body</u>.

Your <u>spirit</u> is the God part of you; your <u>soul</u> is your mind, will, and emotions; and your body is your body.

> *For anyone who speaks in a tongue does not speak to men but to God. Indeed, no one understands him; <u>he utters mysteries with his spirit</u>.*
>
> —1 Corinthians 14:2

What is "revelation"? <u>When our minds pick up on the thoughts of God as our spirits pick up on the thoughts of God</u>.

First Corinthians 2:16 says you have <u>the mind of Christ</u>.

You have the ability, by praying in the Spirit (tongues), to receive <u>mysteries</u>, things you didn't know; and by that knowledge, you're able to make right judgments or decisions about <u>all</u> things!

The Baptism of the Holy Spirit is God's <u>secret weapon</u>—how He can download His will into the earth realm without the devil knowing what is going on.

Praying in the Spirit:
- Is part of your spiritual <u>armor</u> (Ephesians 6:18).
- Allows you to pick up on <u>strategies</u> that will help you sidestep the enemy, or advance with unique and unusual tactics.
- Helps you make the right <u>decisions</u> in life by tapping into the mind of Christ.

Chapter 7

The Kingdom operates by <u>laws</u>, not favors. God doesn't play favorites.

> *Thus says the Lord, your Redeemer, The Holy One of Israel: "I am the Lord your God, Who <u>teaches you to profit</u>, Who <u>leads you by the way you should go</u>."*
>
> —Isaiah 48:17 (NKJV)

There is nothing more powerful than having the <u>plan</u>. Without the plan, the picture is a dream. But with the plan, the dream can be <u>built</u>.

> *The kingdom of God does not come with your careful observation, nor will they say, "Here it is," or "There it is," because the kingdom of God is <u>within you</u>.*
>
> —Luke 17:20-21

Typically, when we need something or need help, we've trained ourselves to look <u>outside</u> of ourselves for the answer. But, now, the Holy Spirit, God Himself, lives <u>in</u> us and is our help.

Why is the Kingdom of God compared to a treasure? <u>Because if you have access to heaven's knowledge, you can know what to do in every situation with unique, unusual, and God-given strategies</u>.

God's secrets are hidden <u>for</u> you, not <u>from</u> you. Satan dwells in darkness and doesn't know the plans of God.

The disciples came to him and asked, "Why do you speak to the people in parables?"

He replied, "The knowledge of the secrets [these things that are hidden] of the kingdom of heaven <u>has been given to you</u>, but not to them."

—Matthew 13:10-11

The Bible says Satan will <u>change tactics</u> if he can pick up on what God is doing.

God is never <u>late</u>. What you see as a delay is working for you by keeping the answer hidden until it's time for it to be revealed.

Why is it important that you don't always act right away on the idea, direction, or plan God gives you? <u>To ensure no one steals it, and to give yourself time to prepare</u>

Once you hear the idea or direction, you must not move on it until you have <u>the capacity to occupy it</u>.

Many times, the Holy Spirit will reveal an idea to us, not revealing it for us to move on the idea at that moment but to allow us to <u>prepare</u> so that we can actually <u>capture the opportunity</u>.

The <u>preparation</u> phase is the most important part of the process.

<u>Preparation</u> and <u>timing</u> are just as important, or more important, than the idea itself!

Chapter 8

What was the result of Daniel being able to hear God's voice? <u>Promotion and wealth</u>

It is the hard place that gives you the perfect opportunity to bring the <u>solution</u>.

The hard place is the perfect setup for your next <u>promotion</u>!

The hard and impossible places are not hard and impossible when <u>you know the answer</u>!

Chapter 9

The normal voice of the Holy Spirit is <u>a gentle whisper</u>.

The conscience is:

- An <u>instinctive knowledge</u> of right and wrong.

- <u>The inner voice of God</u> within each person.

- What speaks on our behalf (<u>defends</u>) or condemns (<u>accuses</u>) us.

- An <u>imprint</u> of the Creator and His requirements to live the lives we were created to live.

No one can <u>escape</u> their conscience, but if a person continues to <u>resist</u> the voice of their conscience, that voice will get quieter and quieter.

Paul warns that ignoring your conscience can <u>shipwreck your life</u>.

If you want to hear God, you need to:

1. Keep your conscience <u>clear of accusations</u>.
2. Be quick to <u>repent</u>.

Chapter 10

<u>Dreams</u> and <u>visions</u> are a very big part of how the Holy Spirit speaks to us. Dreams are pictures we see when we're <u>asleep</u>, and visions are pictures we see when we're <u>awake</u>.

Dreams are the <u>voice</u> of the Holy Spirit.

You have to <u>discern</u> dreams.

One more method that God uses to help direct strategy is <u>the gift of prophecy</u>.

According to Paul, prophecy is only to <u>confirm</u> direction, not to <u>give</u> direction.

Chapter 11

You can only walk with authority as you are <u>submitted to authority</u>.

How do you know if you can be trusted with authority? <u>The evidence is in your submission.</u>

Why was Saul disqualified as king? <u>Because he didn't submit to authority.</u>

What does it mean to be "after God's heart"? <u>To hate what God hates and love what God loves; to do what God would have done if He were there; hate sin; and be obedient</u>

Being obedient is spiritual <u>worship</u>.

Everyone must pass the <u>submission</u> test.

<u>Obedience</u> is better than sacrifice.

Learning to respect and honor authority starts <u>at home</u>.

God is your promoter, but He doesn't promote on <u>performance</u> alone. Your <u>integrity</u> has to be tested as well.

> *Slaves, obey your earthly masters with respect and fear, and with sincerity of heart, just as you would obey Christ. <u>Obey them</u> not only to win their favor when their eye is on you, but as slaves of Christ, doing the will of God from your heart. <u>Serve wholeheartedly</u>, as if you were serving the Lord, not*

men, because you know that the Lord will reward everyone for whatever good he does, whether he is slave or free.

And masters, treat your slaves in the same way. Do not threaten them, since you know that he who is both their Master and yours is in heaven, and there is no favoritism with him.

—Ephesians 6:5-9